Movie Viewing LOGBOOK

LOGBOOK INFORMATION

Start Date	
End Date	

OWNER INFORMATION

Name	
Address	
Phone Number	
Email Address	

TITLE	

DIRECTOR		YEAR	
LENGTH		SERIES (YES / NO)	
GENRE		SUBJECT	
ACTORS			

OVERALL RATING									
1	2	3	4	5	6	7	8	9	10

MY QUICK REVIEW / NOTES

TITLE	

DIRECTOR		YEAR	
LENGTH		SERIES (YES / NO)	
GENRE		SUBJECT	
ACTORS			

OVERALL RATING									
1	2	3	4	5	6	7	8	9	10

MY QUICK REVIEW / NOTES

TITLE	

DIRECTOR		YEAR	
LENGTH		SERIES (YES / NO)	
GENRE		SUBJECT	
ACTORS			

OVERALL RATING									
1	2	3	4	5	6	7	8	9	10

MY QUICK REVIEW / NOTES

TITLE	

DIRECTOR		YEAR	
LENGTH		SERIES (YES / NO)	
GENRE		SUBJECT	
ACTORS			

OVERALL RATING									
1	2	3	4	5	6	7	8	9	10

MY QUICK REVIEW / NOTES

TITLE	

DIRECTOR		YEAR	
LENGTH		SERIES (YES / NO)	
GENRE		SUBJECT	
ACTORS			

OVERALL RATING

1	2	3	4	5	6	7	8	9	10

MY QUICK REVIEW / NOTES

....
....
....

TITLE	

DIRECTOR		YEAR	
LENGTH		SERIES (YES / NO)	
GENRE		SUBJECT	
ACTORS			

OVERALL RATING

1	2	3	4	5	6	7	8	9	10

MY QUICK REVIEW / NOTES

....
....
....

TITLE	

DIRECTOR		YEAR	
LENGTH		SERIES (YES / NO)	
GENRE		SUBJECT	
ACTORS			

OVERALL RATING

1	2	3	4	5	6	7	8	9	10

MY QUICK REVIEW / NOTES

....

....

....

....

TITLE	

DIRECTOR		YEAR	
LENGTH		SERIES (YES / NO)	
GENRE		SUBJECT	
ACTORS			

OVERALL RATING

1	2	3	4	5	6	7	8	9	10

MY QUICK REVIEW / NOTES

....

....

....

....

TITLE	

DIRECTOR		YEAR	
LENGTH		SERIES (YES / NO)	
GENRE		SUBJECT	
ACTORS			

OVERALL RATING

1	2	3	4	5	6	7	8	9	10

MY QUICK REVIEW / NOTES

....
....
....
....

TITLE	

DIRECTOR		YEAR	
LENGTH		SERIES (YES / NO)	
GENRE		SUBJECT	
ACTORS			

OVERALL RATING

1	2	3	4	5	6	7	8	9	10

MY QUICK REVIEW / NOTES

....
....
....
....

TITLE	

DIRECTOR		YEAR	
LENGTH		SERIES (YES / NO)	
GENRE		SUBJECT	
ACTORS			

OVERALL RATING									
1	2	3	4	5	6	7	8	9	10

MY QUICK REVIEW / NOTES

....
....
....
....

TITLE	

DIRECTOR		YEAR	
LENGTH		SERIES (YES / NO)	
GENRE		SUBJECT	
ACTORS			

OVERALL RATING									
1	2	3	4	5	6	7	8	9	10

MY QUICK REVIEW / NOTES

....
....
....
....

TITLE	

DIRECTOR		YEAR	
LENGTH		SERIES (YES / NO)	
GENRE		SUBJECT	
ACTORS			

OVERALL RATING									
1	2	3	4	5	6	7	8	9	10

MY QUICK REVIEW / NOTES

....
....
....

TITLE	

DIRECTOR		YEAR	
LENGTH		SERIES (YES / NO)	
GENRE		SUBJECT	
ACTORS			

OVERALL RATING									
1	2	3	4	5	6	7	8	9	10

MY QUICK REVIEW / NOTES

....
....
....

TITLE	

DIRECTOR		YEAR	
LENGTH		SERIES (YES / NO)	
GENRE		SUBJECT	
ACTORS			

OVERALL RATING									
1	2	3	4	5	6	7	8	9	10

MY QUICK REVIEW / NOTES

TITLE	

DIRECTOR		YEAR	
LENGTH		SERIES (YES / NO)	
GENRE		SUBJECT	
ACTORS			

OVERALL RATING									
1	2	3	4	5	6	7	8	9	10

MY QUICK REVIEW / NOTES

TITLE	

DIRECTOR		YEAR	
LENGTH		SERIES (YES / NO)	
GENRE		SUBJECT	
ACTORS			

OVERALL RATING									
1	2	3	4	5	6	7	8	9	10

MY QUICK REVIEW / NOTES

....

....

....

TITLE	

DIRECTOR		YEAR	
LENGTH		SERIES (YES / NO)	
GENRE		SUBJECT	
ACTORS			

OVERALL RATING									
1	2	3	4	5	6	7	8	9	10

MY QUICK REVIEW / NOTES

....

....

....

TITLE	

DIRECTOR		YEAR	
LENGTH		SERIES (YES / NO)	
GENRE		SUBJECT	
ACTORS			

OVERALL RATING

1	2	3	4	5	6	7	8	9	10

MY QUICK REVIEW / NOTES

....

....

....

....

TITLE	

DIRECTOR		YEAR	
LENGTH		SERIES (YES / NO)	
GENRE		SUBJECT	
ACTORS			

OVERALL RATING

1	2	3	4	5	6	7	8	9	10

MY QUICK REVIEW / NOTES

....

....

....

....

TITLE	

DIRECTOR		YEAR	
LENGTH		SERIES (YES / NO)	
GENRE		SUBJECT	
ACTORS			

OVERALL RATING									
1	2	3	4	5	6	7	8	9	10

MY QUICK REVIEW / NOTES

....

....

....

TITLE	

DIRECTOR		YEAR	
LENGTH		SERIES (YES / NO)	
GENRE		SUBJECT	
ACTORS			

OVERALL RATING									
1	2	3	4	5	6	7	8	9	10

MY QUICK REVIEW / NOTES

....

....

....

TITLE	

DIRECTOR		YEAR	
LENGTH		SERIES (YES / NO)	
GENRE		SUBJECT	
ACTORS			

OVERALL RATING									
1	2	3	4	5	6	7	8	9	10

MY QUICK REVIEW / NOTES
....
....
....
....

TITLE	

DIRECTOR		YEAR	
LENGTH		SERIES (YES / NO)	
GENRE		SUBJECT	
ACTORS			

OVERALL RATING									
1	2	3	4	5	6	7	8	9	10

MY QUICK REVIEW / NOTES
....
....
....
....

TITLE	

DIRECTOR		YEAR	
LENGTH		SERIES (YES / NO)	
GENRE		SUBJECT	
ACTORS			

OVERALL RATING

1	2	3	4	5	6	7	8	9	10

MY QUICK REVIEW / NOTES

TITLE	

DIRECTOR		YEAR	
LENGTH		SERIES (YES / NO)	
GENRE		SUBJECT	
ACTORS			

OVERALL RATING

1	2	3	4	5	6	7	8	9	10

MY QUICK REVIEW / NOTES

TITLE	

DIRECTOR		YEAR	
LENGTH		SERIES (YES / NO)	
GENRE		SUBJECT	
ACTORS			

OVERALL RATING

1	2	3	4	5	6	7	8	9	10

MY QUICK REVIEW / NOTES

....
....
....
....

TITLE	

DIRECTOR		YEAR	
LENGTH		SERIES (YES / NO)	
GENRE		SUBJECT	
ACTORS			

OVERALL RATING

1	2	3	4	5	6	7	8	9	10

MY QUICK REVIEW / NOTES

....
....
....
....

TITLE	

DIRECTOR		YEAR	
LENGTH		SERIES (YES / NO)	
GENRE		SUBJECT	
ACTORS			

OVERALL RATING									
1	2	3	4	5	6	7	8	9	10

MY QUICK REVIEW / NOTES

TITLE	

DIRECTOR		YEAR	
LENGTH		SERIES (YES / NO)	
GENRE		SUBJECT	
ACTORS			

OVERALL RATING									
1	2	3	4	5	6	7	8	9	10

MY QUICK REVIEW / NOTES

TITLE	

DIRECTOR		YEAR	
LENGTH		SERIES (YES / NO)	
GENRE		SUBJECT	
ACTORS			

OVERALL RATING

1	2	3	4	5	6	7	8	9	10

MY QUICK REVIEW / NOTES

....
....
....
....

TITLE	

DIRECTOR		YEAR	
LENGTH		SERIES (YES / NO)	
GENRE		SUBJECT	
ACTORS			

OVERALL RATING

1	2	3	4	5	6	7	8	9	10

MY QUICK REVIEW / NOTES

....
....
....
....

TITLE	

DIRECTOR		YEAR	
LENGTH		SERIES (YES / NO)	
GENRE		SUBJECT	
ACTORS			

OVERALL RATING									
1	2	3	4	5	6	7	8	9	10

MY QUICK REVIEW / NOTES

....
....
....

TITLE	

DIRECTOR		YEAR	
LENGTH		SERIES (YES / NO)	
GENRE		SUBJECT	
ACTORS			

OVERALL RATING									
1	2	3	4	5	6	7	8	9	10

MY QUICK REVIEW / NOTES

....
....
....

TITLE	

DIRECTOR		YEAR	
LENGTH		SERIES (YES / NO)	
GENRE		SUBJECT	
ACTORS			

OVERALL RATING									
1	2	3	4	5	6	7	8	9	10

MY QUICK REVIEW / NOTES

TITLE	

DIRECTOR		YEAR	
LENGTH		SERIES (YES / NO)	
GENRE		SUBJECT	
ACTORS			

OVERALL RATING									
1	2	3	4	5	6	7	8	9	10

MY QUICK REVIEW / NOTES

TITLE	

DIRECTOR		YEAR	
LENGTH		SERIES (YES / NO)	
GENRE		SUBJECT	
ACTORS			

OVERALL RATING									
1	2	3	4	5	6	7	8	9	10

MY QUICK REVIEW / NOTES

TITLE	

DIRECTOR		YEAR	
LENGTH		SERIES (YES / NO)	
GENRE		SUBJECT	
ACTORS			

OVERALL RATING									
1	2	3	4	5	6	7	8	9	10

MY QUICK REVIEW / NOTES

TITLE	

DIRECTOR		YEAR	
LENGTH		SERIES (YES / NO)	
GENRE		SUBJECT	
ACTORS			

OVERALL RATING

1	2	3	4	5	6	7	8	9	10

MY QUICK REVIEW / NOTES

....

....

....

....

TITLE	

DIRECTOR		YEAR	
LENGTH		SERIES (YES / NO)	
GENRE		SUBJECT	
ACTORS			

OVERALL RATING

1	2	3	4	5	6	7	8	9	10

MY QUICK REVIEW / NOTES

....

....

....

....

TITLE	

DIRECTOR		YEAR	
LENGTH		SERIES (YES / NO)	
GENRE		SUBJECT	
ACTORS			

OVERALL RATING

1	2	3	4	5	6	7	8	9	10

MY QUICK REVIEW / NOTES

....
....
....
....

TITLE	

DIRECTOR		YEAR	
LENGTH		SERIES (YES / NO)	
GENRE		SUBJECT	
ACTORS			

OVERALL RATING

1	2	3	4	5	6	7	8	9	10

MY QUICK REVIEW / NOTES

....
....
....
....

TITLE	

DIRECTOR		YEAR	
LENGTH		SERIES (YES / NO)	
GENRE		SUBJECT	
ACTORS			

OVERALL RATING

1	2	3	4	5	6	7	8	9	10

MY QUICK REVIEW / NOTES

....
....
....
....

TITLE	

DIRECTOR		YEAR	
LENGTH		SERIES (YES / NO)	
GENRE		SUBJECT	
ACTORS			

OVERALL RATING

1	2	3	4	5	6	7	8	9	10

MY QUICK REVIEW / NOTES

....
....
....
....

TITLE	

DIRECTOR		YEAR	
LENGTH		SERIES (YES / NO)	
GENRE		SUBJECT	
ACTORS			

OVERALL RATING

1	2	3	4	5	6	7	8	9	10

MY QUICK REVIEW / NOTES

....
....
....

TITLE	

DIRECTOR		YEAR	
LENGTH		SERIES (YES / NO)	
GENRE		SUBJECT	
ACTORS			

OVERALL RATING

1	2	3	4	5	6	7	8	9	10

MY QUICK REVIEW / NOTES

....
....
....

TITLE	

DIRECTOR		YEAR	
LENGTH		SERIES (YES / NO)	
GENRE		SUBJECT	
ACTORS			

OVERALL RATING									
1	2	3	4	5	6	7	8	9	10

MY QUICK REVIEW / NOTES

TITLE	

DIRECTOR		YEAR	
LENGTH		SERIES (YES / NO)	
GENRE		SUBJECT	
ACTORS			

OVERALL RATING									
1	2	3	4	5	6	7	8	9	10

MY QUICK REVIEW / NOTES

TITLE	

DIRECTOR		YEAR	
LENGTH		SERIES (YES / NO)	
GENRE		SUBJECT	
ACTORS			

OVERALL RATING

1	2	3	4	5	6	7	8	9	10

MY QUICK REVIEW / NOTES

....
....
....

TITLE	

DIRECTOR		YEAR	
LENGTH		SERIES (YES / NO)	
GENRE		SUBJECT	
ACTORS			

OVERALL RATING

1	2	3	4	5	6	7	8	9	10

MY QUICK REVIEW / NOTES

....
....
....

TITLE	

DIRECTOR		YEAR	
LENGTH		SERIES (YES / NO)	
GENRE		SUBJECT	
ACTORS			

OVERALL RATING

1	2	3	4	5	6	7	8	9	10

MY QUICK REVIEW / NOTES

....
....
....
....

TITLE	

DIRECTOR		YEAR	
LENGTH		SERIES (YES / NO)	
GENRE		SUBJECT	
ACTORS			

OVERALL RATING

1	2	3	4	5	6	7	8	9	10

MY QUICK REVIEW / NOTES

....
....
....
....

TITLE	

DIRECTOR		YEAR	
LENGTH		SERIES (YES / NO)	
GENRE		SUBJECT	
ACTORS			

OVERALL RATING									
1	2	3	4	5	6	7	8	9	10

MY QUICK REVIEW / NOTES

TITLE	

DIRECTOR		YEAR	
LENGTH		SERIES (YES / NO)	
GENRE		SUBJECT	
ACTORS			

OVERALL RATING									
1	2	3	4	5	6	7	8	9	10

MY QUICK REVIEW / NOTES

TITLE	

DIRECTOR		YEAR	
LENGTH		SERIES (YES / NO)	
GENRE		SUBJECT	
ACTORS			

OVERALL RATING

1	2	3	4	5	6	7	8	9	10

MY QUICK REVIEW / NOTES

TITLE	

DIRECTOR		YEAR	
LENGTH		SERIES (YES / NO)	
GENRE		SUBJECT	
ACTORS			

OVERALL RATING

1	2	3	4	5	6	7	8	9	10

MY QUICK REVIEW / NOTES

TITLE	

DIRECTOR		YEAR	
LENGTH		SERIES (YES / NO)	
GENRE		SUBJECT	
ACTORS			

OVERALL RATING

1	2	3	4	5	6	7	8	9	10

MY QUICK REVIEW / NOTES

....
....
....

TITLE	

DIRECTOR		YEAR	
LENGTH		SERIES (YES / NO)	
GENRE		SUBJECT	
ACTORS			

OVERALL RATING

1	2	3	4	5	6	7	8	9	10

MY QUICK REVIEW / NOTES

....
....
....

TITLE	

DIRECTOR		YEAR	
LENGTH		SERIES (YES / NO)	
GENRE		SUBJECT	
ACTORS			

OVERALL RATING

1	2	3	4	5	6	7	8	9	10

MY QUICK REVIEW / NOTES

....
....
....
....

TITLE	

DIRECTOR		YEAR	
LENGTH		SERIES (YES / NO)	
GENRE		SUBJECT	
ACTORS			

OVERALL RATING

1	2	3	4	5	6	7	8	9	10

MY QUICK REVIEW / NOTES

....
....
....
....

TITLE	

DIRECTOR		YEAR	
LENGTH		SERIES (YES / NO)	
GENRE		SUBJECT	
ACTORS			

OVERALL RATING									
1	2	3	4	5	6	7	8	9	10

MY QUICK REVIEW / NOTES

....
....
....
....

TITLE	

DIRECTOR		YEAR	
LENGTH		SERIES (YES / NO)	
GENRE		SUBJECT	
ACTORS			

OVERALL RATING									
1	2	3	4	5	6	7	8	9	10

MY QUICK REVIEW / NOTES

....
....
....
....

TITLE	

DIRECTOR		YEAR	
LENGTH		SERIES (YES / NO)	
GENRE		SUBJECT	
ACTORS			

OVERALL RATING

1	2	3	4	5	6	7	8	9	10

MY QUICK REVIEW / NOTES

....

....

....

....

TITLE	

DIRECTOR		YEAR	
LENGTH		SERIES (YES / NO)	
GENRE		SUBJECT	
ACTORS			

OVERALL RATING

1	2	3	4	5	6	7	8	9	10

MY QUICK REVIEW / NOTES

....

....

....

....

TITLE	

DIRECTOR		YEAR	
LENGTH		SERIES (YES / NO)	
GENRE		SUBJECT	
ACTORS			

OVERALL RATING									
1	2	3	4	5	6	7	8	9	10

MY QUICK REVIEW / NOTES

TITLE	

DIRECTOR		YEAR	
LENGTH		SERIES (YES / NO)	
GENRE		SUBJECT	
ACTORS			

OVERALL RATING									
1	2	3	4	5	6	7	8	9	10

MY QUICK REVIEW / NOTES

TITLE	

DIRECTOR		YEAR	
LENGTH		SERIES (YES / NO)	
GENRE		SUBJECT	
ACTORS			

OVERALL RATING

1	2	3	4	5	6	7	8	9	10

MY QUICK REVIEW / NOTES

....
....
....

TITLE	

DIRECTOR		YEAR	
LENGTH		SERIES (YES / NO)	
GENRE		SUBJECT	
ACTORS			

OVERALL RATING

1	2	3	4	5	6	7	8	9	10

MY QUICK REVIEW / NOTES

....
....
....

TITLE	

DIRECTOR		YEAR	
LENGTH		SERIES (YES / NO)	
GENRE		SUBJECT	
ACTORS			

OVERALL RATING

1	2	3	4	5	6	7	8	9	10

MY QUICK REVIEW / NOTES

....
....
....

TITLE	

DIRECTOR		YEAR	
LENGTH		SERIES (YES / NO)	
GENRE		SUBJECT	
ACTORS			

OVERALL RATING

1	2	3	4	5	6	7	8	9	10

MY QUICK REVIEW / NOTES

....
....
....

TITLE	

DIRECTOR		YEAR	
LENGTH		SERIES (YES / NO)	
GENRE		SUBJECT	
ACTORS			

OVERALL RATING

1	2	3	4	5	6	7	8	9	10

MY QUICK REVIEW / NOTES

....

....

....

....

TITLE	

DIRECTOR		YEAR	
LENGTH		SERIES (YES / NO)	
GENRE		SUBJECT	
ACTORS			

OVERALL RATING

1	2	3	4	5	6	7	8	9	10

MY QUICK REVIEW / NOTES

....

....

....

....

TITLE	

DIRECTOR		YEAR	
LENGTH		SERIES (YES / NO)	
GENRE		SUBJECT	
ACTORS			

OVERALL RATING									
1	2	3	4	5	6	7	8	9	10

MY QUICK REVIEW / NOTES

....
....
....

TITLE	

DIRECTOR		YEAR	
LENGTH		SERIES (YES / NO)	
GENRE		SUBJECT	
ACTORS			

OVERALL RATING									
1	2	3	4	5	6	7	8	9	10

MY QUICK REVIEW / NOTES

....
....
....

TITLE	

DIRECTOR		YEAR	
LENGTH		SERIES (YES / NO)	
GENRE		SUBJECT	
ACTORS			

OVERALL RATING

1	2	3	4	5	6	7	8	9	10

MY QUICK REVIEW / NOTES

....
....
....
....

TITLE	

DIRECTOR		YEAR	
LENGTH		SERIES (YES / NO)	
GENRE		SUBJECT	
ACTORS			

OVERALL RATING

1	2	3	4	5	6	7	8	9	10

MY QUICK REVIEW / NOTES

....
....
....
....

TITLE	

DIRECTOR		YEAR	
LENGTH		SERIES (YES / NO)	
GENRE		SUBJECT	
ACTORS			

OVERALL RATING

1	2	3	4	5	6	7	8	9	10

MY QUICK REVIEW / NOTES

....

....

....

....

TITLE	

DIRECTOR		YEAR	
LENGTH		SERIES (YES / NO)	
GENRE		SUBJECT	
ACTORS			

OVERALL RATING

1	2	3	4	5	6	7	8	9	10

MY QUICK REVIEW / NOTES

....

....

....

....

TITLE	

DIRECTOR		YEAR	
LENGTH		SERIES (YES / NO)	
GENRE		SUBJECT	
ACTORS			

OVERALL RATING									
1	2	3	4	5	6	7	8	9	10

MY QUICK REVIEW / NOTES

TITLE	

DIRECTOR		YEAR	
LENGTH		SERIES (YES / NO)	
GENRE		SUBJECT	
ACTORS			

OVERALL RATING									
1	2	3	4	5	6	7	8	9	10

MY QUICK REVIEW / NOTES

TITLE	

DIRECTOR		YEAR	
LENGTH		SERIES (YES / NO)	
GENRE		SUBJECT	
ACTORS			

OVERALL RATING

1	2	3	4	5	6	7	8	9	10

MY QUICK REVIEW / NOTES

....
....
....

TITLE	

DIRECTOR		YEAR	
LENGTH		SERIES (YES / NO)	
GENRE		SUBJECT	
ACTORS			

OVERALL RATING

1	2	3	4	5	6	7	8	9	10

MY QUICK REVIEW / NOTES

....
....
....

TITLE	

DIRECTOR		YEAR	
LENGTH		SERIES (YES / NO)	
GENRE		SUBJECT	
ACTORS			

OVERALL RATING

1	2	3	4	5	6	7	8	9	10

MY QUICK REVIEW / NOTES

....
....
....
....

TITLE	

DIRECTOR		YEAR	
LENGTH		SERIES (YES / NO)	
GENRE		SUBJECT	
ACTORS			

OVERALL RATING

1	2	3	4	5	6	7	8	9	10

MY QUICK REVIEW / NOTES

....
....
....
....

TITLE	

DIRECTOR		YEAR	
LENGTH		SERIES (YES / NO)	
GENRE		SUBJECT	
ACTORS			

OVERALL RATING									
1	2	3	4	5	6	7	8	9	10

MY QUICK REVIEW / NOTES

TITLE	

DIRECTOR		YEAR	
LENGTH		SERIES (YES / NO)	
GENRE		SUBJECT	
ACTORS			

OVERALL RATING									
1	2	3	4	5	6	7	8	9	10

MY QUICK REVIEW / NOTES

TITLE	

DIRECTOR		YEAR	
LENGTH		SERIES (YES / NO)	
GENRE		SUBJECT	
ACTORS			

OVERALL RATING									
1	2	3	4	5	6	7	8	9	10

MY QUICK REVIEW / NOTES

....

....

....

....

TITLE	

DIRECTOR		YEAR	
LENGTH		SERIES (YES / NO)	
GENRE		SUBJECT	
ACTORS			

OVERALL RATING									
1	2	3	4	5	6	7	8	9	10

MY QUICK REVIEW / NOTES

....

....

....

....

TITLE	

DIRECTOR		YEAR	
LENGTH		SERIES (YES / NO)	
GENRE		SUBJECT	
ACTORS			

OVERALL RATING									
1	2	3	4	5	6	7	8	9	10

MY QUICK REVIEW / NOTES

....

....

....

....

TITLE	

DIRECTOR		YEAR	
LENGTH		SERIES (YES / NO)	
GENRE		SUBJECT	
ACTORS			

OVERALL RATING									
1	2	3	4	5	6	7	8	9	10

MY QUICK REVIEW / NOTES

....

....

....

....

TITLE	

DIRECTOR		YEAR	
LENGTH		SERIES (YES / NO)	
GENRE		SUBJECT	
ACTORS			

OVERALL RATING

1	2	3	4	5	6	7	8	9	10

MY QUICK REVIEW / NOTES

....
....
....
....

TITLE	

DIRECTOR		YEAR	
LENGTH		SERIES (YES / NO)	
GENRE		SUBJECT	
ACTORS			

OVERALL RATING

1	2	3	4	5	6	7	8	9	10

MY QUICK REVIEW / NOTES

....
....
....
....

TITLE	

DIRECTOR		YEAR	
LENGTH		SERIES (YES / NO)	
GENRE		SUBJECT	
ACTORS			

OVERALL RATING

1	2	3	4	5	6	7	8	9	10

MY QUICK REVIEW / NOTES

....

....

....

TITLE	

DIRECTOR		YEAR	
LENGTH		SERIES (YES / NO)	
GENRE		SUBJECT	
ACTORS			

OVERALL RATING

1	2	3	4	5	6	7	8	9	10

MY QUICK REVIEW / NOTES

....

....

....

TITLE	

DIRECTOR		YEAR	
LENGTH		SERIES (YES / NO)	
GENRE		SUBJECT	
ACTORS			

OVERALL RATING

1	2	3	4	5	6	7	8	9	10

MY QUICK REVIEW / NOTES

....
....
....
....

TITLE	

DIRECTOR		YEAR	
LENGTH		SERIES (YES / NO)	
GENRE		SUBJECT	
ACTORS			

OVERALL RATING

1	2	3	4	5	6	7	8	9	10

MY QUICK REVIEW / NOTES

....
....
....
....

TITLE	

DIRECTOR		YEAR	
LENGTH		SERIES (YES / NO)	
GENRE		SUBJECT	
ACTORS			

OVERALL RATING									
1	2	3	4	5	6	7	8	9	10

MY QUICK REVIEW / NOTES

TITLE	

DIRECTOR		YEAR	
LENGTH		SERIES (YES / NO)	
GENRE		SUBJECT	
ACTORS			

OVERALL RATING									
1	2	3	4	5	6	7	8	9	10

MY QUICK REVIEW / NOTES

TITLE	

DIRECTOR		YEAR	
LENGTH		SERIES (YES / NO)	
GENRE		SUBJECT	
ACTORS			

OVERALL RATING									
1	2	3	4	5	6	7	8	9	10

MY QUICK REVIEW / NOTES

TITLE	

DIRECTOR		YEAR	
LENGTH		SERIES (YES / NO)	
GENRE		SUBJECT	
ACTORS			

OVERALL RATING									
1	2	3	4	5	6	7	8	9	10

MY QUICK REVIEW / NOTES

TITLE	

DIRECTOR		YEAR	
LENGTH		SERIES (YES / NO)	
GENRE		SUBJECT	
ACTORS			

OVERALL RATING									
1	2	3	4	5	6	7	8	9	10

MY QUICK REVIEW / NOTES

....
....
....

TITLE	

DIRECTOR		YEAR	
LENGTH		SERIES (YES / NO)	
GENRE		SUBJECT	
ACTORS			

OVERALL RATING									
1	2	3	4	5	6	7	8	9	10

MY QUICK REVIEW / NOTES

....
....
....

TITLE	

DIRECTOR		YEAR	
LENGTH		SERIES (YES / NO)	
GENRE		SUBJECT	
ACTORS			

OVERALL RATING

1	2	3	4	5	6	7	8	9	10

MY QUICK REVIEW / NOTES

....
....
....
....

TITLE	

DIRECTOR		YEAR	
LENGTH		SERIES (YES / NO)	
GENRE		SUBJECT	
ACTORS			

OVERALL RATING

1	2	3	4	5	6	7	8	9	10

MY QUICK REVIEW / NOTES

....
....
....
....

TITLE	

DIRECTOR		YEAR	
LENGTH		SERIES (YES / NO)	
GENRE		SUBJECT	
ACTORS			

OVERALL RATING

1	2	3	4	5	6	7	8	9	10

MY QUICK REVIEW / NOTES

....
....
....

TITLE	

DIRECTOR		YEAR	
LENGTH		SERIES (YES / NO)	
GENRE		SUBJECT	
ACTORS			

OVERALL RATING

1	2	3	4	5	6	7	8	9	10

MY QUICK REVIEW / NOTES

....
....
....

TITLE	

DIRECTOR		YEAR	
LENGTH		SERIES (YES / NO)	
GENRE		SUBJECT	
ACTORS			

OVERALL RATING

1	2	3	4	5	6	7	8	9	10

MY QUICK REVIEW / NOTES

....

....

....

TITLE	

DIRECTOR		YEAR	
LENGTH		SERIES (YES / NO)	
GENRE		SUBJECT	
ACTORS			

OVERALL RATING

1	2	3	4	5	6	7	8	9	10

MY QUICK REVIEW / NOTES

....

....

....

TITLE	

DIRECTOR		YEAR	
LENGTH		SERIES (YES / NO)	
GENRE		SUBJECT	
ACTORS			

OVERALL RATING									
1	2	3	4	5	6	7	8	9	10

MY QUICK REVIEW / NOTES

TITLE	

DIRECTOR		YEAR	
LENGTH		SERIES (YES / NO)	
GENRE		SUBJECT	
ACTORS			

OVERALL RATING									
1	2	3	4	5	6	7	8	9	10

MY QUICK REVIEW / NOTES

TITLE	

DIRECTOR		YEAR	
LENGTH		SERIES (YES / NO)	
GENRE		SUBJECT	
ACTORS			

OVERALL RATING

1	2	3	4	5	6	7	8	9	10

MY QUICK REVIEW / NOTES

....
....
....
....

TITLE	

DIRECTOR		YEAR	
LENGTH		SERIES (YES / NO)	
GENRE		SUBJECT	
ACTORS			

OVERALL RATING

1	2	3	4	5	6	7	8	9	10

MY QUICK REVIEW / NOTES

....
....
....
....

TITLE	

DIRECTOR		YEAR	
LENGTH		SERIES (YES / NO)	
GENRE		SUBJECT	
ACTORS			

OVERALL RATING

1	2	3	4	5	6	7	8	9	10

MY QUICK REVIEW / NOTES

....
....
....

TITLE	

DIRECTOR		YEAR	
LENGTH		SERIES (YES / NO)	
GENRE		SUBJECT	
ACTORS			

OVERALL RATING

1	2	3	4	5	6	7	8	9	10

MY QUICK REVIEW / NOTES

....
....
....

TITLE	

DIRECTOR		YEAR	
LENGTH		SERIES (YES / NO)	
GENRE		SUBJECT	
ACTORS			

OVERALL RATING									
1	2	3	4	5	6	7	8	9	10

MY QUICK REVIEW / NOTES

....
....
....
....

TITLE	

DIRECTOR		YEAR	
LENGTH		SERIES (YES / NO)	
GENRE		SUBJECT	
ACTORS			

OVERALL RATING									
1	2	3	4	5	6	7	8	9	10

MY QUICK REVIEW / NOTES

....
....
....
....

TITLE	

DIRECTOR		YEAR	
LENGTH		SERIES (YES / NO)	
GENRE		SUBJECT	
ACTORS			

OVERALL RATING

1	2	3	4	5	6	7	8	9	10

MY QUICK REVIEW / NOTES

....
....
....
....

TITLE	

DIRECTOR		YEAR	
LENGTH		SERIES (YES / NO)	
GENRE		SUBJECT	
ACTORS			

OVERALL RATING

1	2	3	4	5	6	7	8	9	10

MY QUICK REVIEW / NOTES

....
....
....
....

TITLE	

DIRECTOR		YEAR	
LENGTH		SERIES (YES / NO)	
GENRE		SUBJECT	
ACTORS			

OVERALL RATING

1	2	3	4	5	6	7	8	9	10

MY QUICK REVIEW / NOTES

....
....
....
....

TITLE	

DIRECTOR		YEAR	
LENGTH		SERIES (YES / NO)	
GENRE		SUBJECT	
ACTORS			

OVERALL RATING

1	2	3	4	5	6	7	8	9	10

MY QUICK REVIEW / NOTES

....
....
....
....

TITLE	

DIRECTOR		YEAR	
LENGTH		SERIES (YES / NO)	
GENRE		SUBJECT	
ACTORS			

OVERALL RATING									
1	2	3	4	5	6	7	8	9	10

MY QUICK REVIEW / NOTES

....
....
....
....

TITLE	

DIRECTOR		YEAR	
LENGTH		SERIES (YES / NO)	
GENRE		SUBJECT	
ACTORS			

OVERALL RATING									
1	2	3	4	5	6	7	8	9	10

MY QUICK REVIEW / NOTES

....
....
....
....

TITLE	

DIRECTOR		YEAR	
LENGTH		SERIES (YES / NO)	
GENRE		SUBJECT	
ACTORS			

OVERALL RATING

1	2	3	4	5	6	7	8	9	10

MY QUICK REVIEW / NOTES

....
....
....
....

TITLE	

DIRECTOR		YEAR	
LENGTH		SERIES (YES / NO)	
GENRE		SUBJECT	
ACTORS			

OVERALL RATING

1	2	3	4	5	6	7	8	9	10

MY QUICK REVIEW / NOTES

....
....
....
....

TITLE	

DIRECTOR		YEAR	
LENGTH		SERIES (YES / NO)	
GENRE		SUBJECT	
ACTORS			

OVERALL RATING									
1	2	3	4	5	6	7	8	9	10

MY QUICK REVIEW / NOTES

....
....
....
....

TITLE	

DIRECTOR		YEAR	
LENGTH		SERIES (YES / NO)	
GENRE		SUBJECT	
ACTORS			

OVERALL RATING									
1	2	3	4	5	6	7	8	9	10

MY QUICK REVIEW / NOTES

....
....
....
....

TITLE	

DIRECTOR		YEAR	
LENGTH		SERIES (YES / NO)	
GENRE		SUBJECT	
ACTORS			

OVERALL RATING

1	2	3	4	5	6	7	8	9	10

MY QUICK REVIEW / NOTES

....
....
....
....

TITLE	

DIRECTOR		YEAR	
LENGTH		SERIES (YES / NO)	
GENRE		SUBJECT	
ACTORS			

OVERALL RATING

1	2	3	4	5	6	7	8	9	10

MY QUICK REVIEW / NOTES

....
....
....
....

TITLE	

DIRECTOR		YEAR	
LENGTH		SERIES (YES / NO)	
GENRE		SUBJECT	
ACTORS			

OVERALL RATING									
1	2	3	4	5	6	7	8	9	10

MY QUICK REVIEW / NOTES

TITLE	

DIRECTOR		YEAR	
LENGTH		SERIES (YES / NO)	
GENRE		SUBJECT	
ACTORS			

OVERALL RATING									
1	2	3	4	5	6	7	8	9	10

MY QUICK REVIEW / NOTES

TITLE	

DIRECTOR		YEAR	
LENGTH		SERIES (YES / NO)	
GENRE		SUBJECT	
ACTORS			

OVERALL RATING									
1	2	3	4	5	6	7	8	9	10

MY QUICK REVIEW / NOTES

....

....

....

....

TITLE	

DIRECTOR		YEAR	
LENGTH		SERIES (YES / NO)	
GENRE		SUBJECT	
ACTORS			

OVERALL RATING									
1	2	3	4	5	6	7	8	9	10

MY QUICK REVIEW / NOTES

....

....

....

....

TITLE	

DIRECTOR		YEAR	
LENGTH		SERIES (YES / NO)	
GENRE		SUBJECT	
ACTORS			

OVERALL RATING

1	2	3	4	5	6	7	8	9	10

MY QUICK REVIEW / NOTES

....
....
....
....

TITLE	

DIRECTOR		YEAR	
LENGTH		SERIES (YES / NO)	
GENRE		SUBJECT	
ACTORS			

OVERALL RATING

1	2	3	4	5	6	7	8	9	10

MY QUICK REVIEW / NOTES

....
....
....
....

TITLE	

DIRECTOR		YEAR	
LENGTH		SERIES (YES / NO)	
GENRE		SUBJECT	
ACTORS			

OVERALL RATING

1	2	3	4	5	6	7	8	9	10

MY QUICK REVIEW / NOTES

....

....

....

....

TITLE	

DIRECTOR		YEAR	
LENGTH		SERIES (YES / NO)	
GENRE		SUBJECT	
ACTORS			

OVERALL RATING

1	2	3	4	5	6	7	8	9	10

MY QUICK REVIEW / NOTES

....

....

....

....

TITLE	

DIRECTOR		YEAR	
LENGTH		SERIES (YES / NO)	
GENRE		SUBJECT	
ACTORS			

OVERALL RATING

1	2	3	4	5	6	7	8	9	10

MY QUICK REVIEW / NOTES

....
....
....
....

TITLE	

DIRECTOR		YEAR	
LENGTH		SERIES (YES / NO)	
GENRE		SUBJECT	
ACTORS			

OVERALL RATING

1	2	3	4	5	6	7	8	9	10

MY QUICK REVIEW / NOTES

....
....
....
....

TITLE	

DIRECTOR		YEAR	
LENGTH		SERIES (YES / NO)	
GENRE		SUBJECT	
ACTORS			

OVERALL RATING

1	2	3	4	5	6	7	8	9	10

MY QUICK REVIEW / NOTES

....
....
....
....

TITLE	

DIRECTOR		YEAR	
LENGTH		SERIES (YES / NO)	
GENRE		SUBJECT	
ACTORS			

OVERALL RATING

1	2	3	4	5	6	7	8	9	10

MY QUICK REVIEW / NOTES

....
....
....
....

TITLE	

DIRECTOR		YEAR	
LENGTH		SERIES (YES / NO)	
GENRE		SUBJECT	
ACTORS			

OVERALL RATING

1	2	3	4	5	6	7	8	9	10

MY QUICK REVIEW / NOTES

....
....
....
....

TITLE	

DIRECTOR		YEAR	
LENGTH		SERIES (YES / NO)	
GENRE		SUBJECT	
ACTORS			

OVERALL RATING

1	2	3	4	5	6	7	8	9	10

MY QUICK REVIEW / NOTES

....
....
....
....

TITLE	

DIRECTOR		YEAR	
LENGTH		SERIES (YES / NO)	
GENRE		SUBJECT	
ACTORS			

OVERALL RATING

1	2	3	4	5	6	7	8	9	10

MY QUICK REVIEW / NOTES

....
....
....

TITLE	

DIRECTOR		YEAR	
LENGTH		SERIES (YES / NO)	
GENRE		SUBJECT	
ACTORS			

OVERALL RATING

1	2	3	4	5	6	7	8	9	10

MY QUICK REVIEW / NOTES

....
....
....

TITLE	

DIRECTOR		YEAR	
LENGTH		SERIES (YES / NO)	
GENRE		SUBJECT	
ACTORS			

OVERALL RATING

1	2	3	4	5	6	7	8	9	10

MY QUICK REVIEW / NOTES

....
....
....
....

TITLE	

DIRECTOR		YEAR	
LENGTH		SERIES (YES / NO)	
GENRE		SUBJECT	
ACTORS			

OVERALL RATING

1	2	3	4	5	6	7	8	9	10

MY QUICK REVIEW / NOTES

....
....
....
....

TITLE	

DIRECTOR		YEAR	
LENGTH		SERIES (YES / NO)	
GENRE		SUBJECT	
ACTORS			

OVERALL RATING									
1	2	3	4	5	6	7	8	9	10

MY QUICK REVIEW / NOTES

....
....
....
....

TITLE	

DIRECTOR		YEAR	
LENGTH		SERIES (YES / NO)	
GENRE		SUBJECT	
ACTORS			

OVERALL RATING									
1	2	3	4	5	6	7	8	9	10

MY QUICK REVIEW / NOTES

....
....
....
....

TITLE	

DIRECTOR		YEAR	
LENGTH		SERIES (YES / NO)	
GENRE		SUBJECT	
ACTORS			

OVERALL RATING

1	2	3	4	5	6	7	8	9	10

MY QUICK REVIEW / NOTES

....
....
....
....

TITLE	

DIRECTOR		YEAR	
LENGTH		SERIES (YES / NO)	
GENRE		SUBJECT	
ACTORS			

OVERALL RATING

1	2	3	4	5	6	7	8	9	10

MY QUICK REVIEW / NOTES

....
....
....
....

TITLE	

DIRECTOR		YEAR	
LENGTH		SERIES (YES / NO)	
GENRE		SUBJECT	
ACTORS			

OVERALL RATING

1	2	3	4	5	6	7	8	9	10

MY QUICK REVIEW / NOTES

....
....
....
....

TITLE	

DIRECTOR		YEAR	
LENGTH		SERIES (YES / NO)	
GENRE		SUBJECT	
ACTORS			

OVERALL RATING

1	2	3	4	5	6	7	8	9	10

MY QUICK REVIEW / NOTES

....
....
....
....

TITLE	

DIRECTOR		YEAR	
LENGTH		SERIES (YES / NO)	
GENRE		SUBJECT	
ACTORS			

OVERALL RATING

1	2	3	4	5	6	7	8	9	10

MY QUICK REVIEW / NOTES

....
....
....
....

TITLE	

DIRECTOR		YEAR	
LENGTH		SERIES (YES / NO)	
GENRE		SUBJECT	
ACTORS			

OVERALL RATING

1	2	3	4	5	6	7	8	9	10

MY QUICK REVIEW / NOTES

....
....
....
....

TITLE	

DIRECTOR		YEAR	
LENGTH		SERIES (YES / NO)	
GENRE		SUBJECT	
ACTORS			

OVERALL RATING

1	2	3	4	5	6	7	8	9	10

MY QUICK REVIEW / NOTES

....
....
....
....

TITLE	

DIRECTOR		YEAR	
LENGTH		SERIES (YES / NO)	
GENRE		SUBJECT	
ACTORS			

OVERALL RATING

1	2	3	4	5	6	7	8	9	10

MY QUICK REVIEW / NOTES

....
....
....
....

TITLE	

DIRECTOR		YEAR	
LENGTH		SERIES (YES / NO)	
GENRE		SUBJECT	
ACTORS			

OVERALL RATING

1	2	3	4	5	6	7	8	9	10

MY QUICK REVIEW / NOTES

....

....

....

....

TITLE	

DIRECTOR		YEAR	
LENGTH		SERIES (YES / NO)	
GENRE		SUBJECT	
ACTORS			

OVERALL RATING

1	2	3	4	5	6	7	8	9	10

MY QUICK REVIEW / NOTES

....

....

....

....

TITLE	

DIRECTOR		YEAR	
LENGTH		SERIES (YES / NO)	
GENRE		SUBJECT	
ACTORS			

OVERALL RATING

1	2	3	4	5	6	7	8	9	10

MY QUICK REVIEW / NOTES

....
....
....
....

TITLE	

DIRECTOR		YEAR	
LENGTH		SERIES (YES / NO)	
GENRE		SUBJECT	
ACTORS			

OVERALL RATING

1	2	3	4	5	6	7	8	9	10

MY QUICK REVIEW / NOTES

....
....
....
....

TITLE	

DIRECTOR		YEAR	
LENGTH		SERIES (YES / NO)	
GENRE		SUBJECT	
ACTORS			

OVERALL RATING									
1	2	3	4	5	6	7	8	9	10

MY QUICK REVIEW / NOTES

TITLE	

DIRECTOR		YEAR	
LENGTH		SERIES (YES / NO)	
GENRE		SUBJECT	
ACTORS			

OVERALL RATING									
1	2	3	4	5	6	7	8	9	10

MY QUICK REVIEW / NOTES

TITLE	

DIRECTOR		YEAR	
LENGTH		SERIES (YES / NO)	
GENRE		SUBJECT	
ACTORS			

OVERALL RATING

1	2	3	4	5	6	7	8	9	10

MY QUICK REVIEW / NOTES

....
....
....
....

TITLE	

DIRECTOR		YEAR	
LENGTH		SERIES (YES / NO)	
GENRE		SUBJECT	
ACTORS			

OVERALL RATING

1	2	3	4	5	6	7	8	9	10

MY QUICK REVIEW / NOTES

....
....
....
....

TITLE	

DIRECTOR		YEAR	
LENGTH		SERIES (YES / NO)	
GENRE		SUBJECT	
ACTORS			

OVERALL RATING

1	2	3	4	5	6	7	8	9	10

MY QUICK REVIEW / NOTES

....

....

....

....

TITLE	

DIRECTOR		YEAR	
LENGTH		SERIES (YES / NO)	
GENRE		SUBJECT	
ACTORS			

OVERALL RATING

1	2	3	4	5	6	7	8	9	10

MY QUICK REVIEW / NOTES

....

....

....

....

TITLE	

DIRECTOR		YEAR	
LENGTH		SERIES (YES / NO)	
GENRE		SUBJECT	
ACTORS			

OVERALL RATING

1	2	3	4	5	6	7	8	9	10

MY QUICK REVIEW / NOTES

....
....
....
....

TITLE	

DIRECTOR		YEAR	
LENGTH		SERIES (YES / NO)	
GENRE		SUBJECT	
ACTORS			

OVERALL RATING

1	2	3	4	5	6	7	8	9	10

MY QUICK REVIEW / NOTES

....
....
....
....

TITLE	

DIRECTOR		YEAR	
LENGTH		SERIES (YES / NO)	
GENRE		SUBJECT	
ACTORS			

OVERALL RATING

1	2	3	4	5	6	7	8	9	10

MY QUICK REVIEW / NOTES

....

....

....

TITLE	

DIRECTOR		YEAR	
LENGTH		SERIES (YES / NO)	
GENRE		SUBJECT	
ACTORS			

OVERALL RATING

1	2	3	4	5	6	7	8	9	10

MY QUICK REVIEW / NOTES

....

....

....

TITLE	

DIRECTOR		YEAR	
LENGTH		SERIES (YES / NO)	
GENRE		SUBJECT	
ACTORS			

OVERALL RATING

1	2	3	4	5	6	7	8	9	10

MY QUICK REVIEW / NOTES

....

....

....

....

TITLE	

DIRECTOR		YEAR	
LENGTH		SERIES (YES / NO)	
GENRE		SUBJECT	
ACTORS			

OVERALL RATING

1	2	3	4	5	6	7	8	9	10

MY QUICK REVIEW / NOTES

....

....

....

....

TITLE	

DIRECTOR		YEAR	
LENGTH		SERIES (YES / NO)	
GENRE		SUBJECT	
ACTORS			

OVERALL RATING

1	2	3	4	5	6	7	8	9	10

MY QUICK REVIEW / NOTES

....
....
....
....

TITLE	

DIRECTOR		YEAR	
LENGTH		SERIES (YES / NO)	
GENRE		SUBJECT	
ACTORS			

OVERALL RATING

1	2	3	4	5	6	7	8	9	10

MY QUICK REVIEW / NOTES

....
....
....
....

TITLE	

DIRECTOR		YEAR	
LENGTH		SERIES (YES / NO)	
GENRE		SUBJECT	
ACTORS			

OVERALL RATING

1	2	3	4	5	6	7	8	9	10

MY QUICK REVIEW / NOTES

....
....
....
....

TITLE	

DIRECTOR		YEAR	
LENGTH		SERIES (YES / NO)	
GENRE		SUBJECT	
ACTORS			

OVERALL RATING

1	2	3	4	5	6	7	8	9	10

MY QUICK REVIEW / NOTES

....
....
....
....

TITLE	

DIRECTOR		YEAR	
LENGTH		SERIES (YES / NO)	
GENRE		SUBJECT	
ACTORS			

OVERALL RATING

1	2	3	4	5	6	7	8	9	10

MY QUICK REVIEW / NOTES

....

....

....

TITLE	

DIRECTOR		YEAR	
LENGTH		SERIES (YES / NO)	
GENRE		SUBJECT	
ACTORS			

OVERALL RATING

1	2	3	4	5	6	7	8	9	10

MY QUICK REVIEW / NOTES

....

....

....

TITLE	

DIRECTOR		YEAR	
LENGTH		SERIES (YES / NO)	
GENRE		SUBJECT	
ACTORS			

OVERALL RATING									
1	2	3	4	5	6	7	8	9	10

MY QUICK REVIEW / NOTES

TITLE	

DIRECTOR		YEAR	
LENGTH		SERIES (YES / NO)	
GENRE		SUBJECT	
ACTORS			

OVERALL RATING									
1	2	3	4	5	6	7	8	9	10

MY QUICK REVIEW / NOTES

TITLE	

DIRECTOR		YEAR	
LENGTH		SERIES (YES / NO)	
GENRE		SUBJECT	
ACTORS			

OVERALL RATING

1	2	3	4	5	6	7	8	9	10

MY QUICK REVIEW / NOTES

....
....
....
....

TITLE	

DIRECTOR		YEAR	
LENGTH		SERIES (YES / NO)	
GENRE		SUBJECT	
ACTORS			

OVERALL RATING

1	2	3	4	5	6	7	8	9	10

MY QUICK REVIEW / NOTES

....
....
....
....

TITLE	

DIRECTOR		YEAR	
LENGTH		SERIES (YES / NO)	
GENRE		SUBJECT	
ACTORS			

OVERALL RATING									
1	2	3	4	5	6	7	8	9	10

MY QUICK REVIEW / NOTES

....
....
....
....

TITLE	

DIRECTOR		YEAR	
LENGTH		SERIES (YES / NO)	
GENRE		SUBJECT	
ACTORS			

OVERALL RATING									
1	2	3	4	5	6	7	8	9	10

MY QUICK REVIEW / NOTES

....
....
....
....

TITLE	

DIRECTOR		YEAR	
LENGTH		SERIES (YES / NO)	
GENRE		SUBJECT	
ACTORS			

OVERALL RATING

1	2	3	4	5	6	7	8	9	10

MY QUICK REVIEW / NOTES

....
....
....
....

TITLE	

DIRECTOR		YEAR	
LENGTH		SERIES (YES / NO)	
GENRE		SUBJECT	
ACTORS			

OVERALL RATING

1	2	3	4	5	6	7	8	9	10

MY QUICK REVIEW / NOTES

....
....
....
....

TITLE	

DIRECTOR		YEAR	
LENGTH		SERIES (YES / NO)	
GENRE		SUBJECT	
ACTORS			

OVERALL RATING									
1	2	3	4	5	6	7	8	9	10

MY QUICK REVIEW / NOTES

TITLE	

DIRECTOR		YEAR	
LENGTH		SERIES (YES / NO)	
GENRE		SUBJECT	
ACTORS			

OVERALL RATING									
1	2	3	4	5	6	7	8	9	10

MY QUICK REVIEW / NOTES

TITLE	

DIRECTOR		YEAR	
LENGTH		SERIES (YES / NO)	
GENRE		SUBJECT	
ACTORS			

OVERALL RATING

1	2	3	4	5	6	7	8	9	10

MY QUICK REVIEW / NOTES

....
....
....
....

TITLE	

DIRECTOR		YEAR	
LENGTH		SERIES (YES / NO)	
GENRE		SUBJECT	
ACTORS			

OVERALL RATING

1	2	3	4	5	6	7	8	9	10

MY QUICK REVIEW / NOTES

....
....
....
....

TITLE	

DIRECTOR		YEAR	
LENGTH		SERIES (YES / NO)	
GENRE		SUBJECT	
ACTORS			

OVERALL RATING

1	2	3	4	5	6	7	8	9	10

MY QUICK REVIEW / NOTES

TITLE	

DIRECTOR		YEAR	
LENGTH		SERIES (YES / NO)	
GENRE		SUBJECT	
ACTORS			

OVERALL RATING

1	2	3	4	5	6	7	8	9	10

MY QUICK REVIEW / NOTES

TITLE	

DIRECTOR		YEAR	
LENGTH		SERIES (YES / NO)	
GENRE		SUBJECT	
ACTORS			

OVERALL RATING									
1	2	3	4	5	6	7	8	9	10

MY QUICK REVIEW / NOTES

....
....
....
....

TITLE	

DIRECTOR		YEAR	
LENGTH		SERIES (YES / NO)	
GENRE		SUBJECT	
ACTORS			

OVERALL RATING									
1	2	3	4	5	6	7	8	9	10

MY QUICK REVIEW / NOTES

....
....
....
....

TITLE	

DIRECTOR		YEAR	
LENGTH		SERIES (YES / NO)	
GENRE		SUBJECT	
ACTORS			

OVERALL RATING									
1	2	3	4	5	6	7	8	9	10

MY QUICK REVIEW / NOTES
....
....
....
....

TITLE	

DIRECTOR		YEAR	
LENGTH		SERIES (YES / NO)	
GENRE		SUBJECT	
ACTORS			

OVERALL RATING									
1	2	3	4	5	6	7	8	9	10

MY QUICK REVIEW / NOTES
....
....
....
....

TITLE	

DIRECTOR		YEAR	
LENGTH		SERIES (YES / NO)	
GENRE		SUBJECT	
ACTORS			

OVERALL RATING

1	2	3	4	5	6	7	8	9	10

MY QUICK REVIEW / NOTES

....
....
....
....

TITLE	

DIRECTOR		YEAR	
LENGTH		SERIES (YES / NO)	
GENRE		SUBJECT	
ACTORS			

OVERALL RATING

1	2	3	4	5	6	7	8	9	10

MY QUICK REVIEW / NOTES

....
....
....
....

TITLE	

DIRECTOR		YEAR	
LENGTH		SERIES (YES / NO)	
GENRE		SUBJECT	
ACTORS			

OVERALL RATING

1	2	3	4	5	6	7	8	9	10

MY QUICK REVIEW / NOTES

....

....

....

TITLE	

DIRECTOR		YEAR	
LENGTH		SERIES (YES / NO)	
GENRE		SUBJECT	
ACTORS			

OVERALL RATING

1	2	3	4	5	6	7	8	9	10

MY QUICK REVIEW / NOTES

....

....

....

TITLE	YEAR	GENRE	RATING	LOG PAGE

TITLE	YEAR	GENRE	RATING	LOG PAGE

TITLE	YEAR	GENRE	RATING	LOG PAGE

TITLE	YEAR	GENRE	RATING	LOG PAGE

TITLE	YEAR	GENRE	RATING	LOG PAGE

TITLE	YEAR	GENRE	RATING	LOG PAGE

TITLE	YEAR	GENRE	RATING	LOG PAGE

TITLE	YEAR	GENRE	RATING	LOG PAGE

Made in the USA
Columbia, SC
20 December 2019